MAIN
CHARACTER
ENERGY

Jordan Paramor

MAIN
CHARACTER
ENERGY

ROMANTICISE YOUR LIFE
and PUT YOURSELF FIRST

wren
&rook

First published in Great Britain in 2023 by Wren & Rook

Cover and inside artwork from Shutterstock.com

ISBN: 978 1 5263 6602 3
eBook ISBN: 978 1 5263 6603 0

3 5 7 9 10 8 6 4 2

Wren & Rook
An imprint of
Hachette Children's Group
Part of Hodder & Stoughton
Carmelite House
50 Victoria Embankment
London EC4Y 0DZ

An Hachette UK Company
www.hachette.co.uk
www.hachettechildrens.co.uk

Printed and bound in Great Britain by Clays Ltd, Elcograf S.p.A.

CONTENTS

INTRODUCTION

Welcome to the ultimate guide to main character energy. If you've heard about it but you're not totally sure what it is, don't worry – explanation coming right up . . .

Q: WHAT IS MAIN CHARACTER ENERGY?

A: It's about you choosing to put yourself first, building your confidence and trying to treat every day like the intro to a romantic comedy – the type where the protagonist is walking down the street with an epic soundtrack and a smile beaming from their face because they're following their dream and nothing can stop them. Channel a bit of main character energy and you can start living life as if you're the protagonist in an epic story.

Q: THAT SOUNDS LIKE A BIG CHANGE – WHERE DO I START?

A: Don't worry – you'll find all the answers you need in this book. Harnessing your main character energy (MCE) is about choosing to live your best life and taking the steps to achieve this goal.

Essentially, if you're not taking the time to prioritise your own goals and wellbeing, then you're depriving the world of your ultimate greatness, and no one wants that.

We all often doubt ourselves. But MCE is about embracing ourselves, faults and all. Because everyone has their own quirky habits and secret guilty pleasures, which are what make them unique. So here are some things to tell yourself if you ever doubt your MCE. You can even look in the mirror and say them to yourself as affirmations:

I am a wonderfully, crazily, endearingly brilliant individual.

There is no one in the world who thinks exactly like me.

I am unique.

I am complete.

CHAPTER 1

FINDING YOUR
MAIN CHARACTER ENERGY

NEW MINDSET, WHO DIS?

The three most important steps when it comes to channelling main character energy are changing your mindset, thinking positively, prioritising yourself and being forward-thinking.

You are the protagonist who is taking control of your life and only doing the things that make you happy. You may be embroiled in a toxic relationship you want out of or looking for new hobbies to do in your spare time. Or maybe you're simply learning to love being in your own company.

It can be hard to feel comfortable in ourselves when we're surrounded by examples of how we 'should' look and feel. MCE is about making choices that work for you and doing things that make you happy and let you nurture your self-worth. Main character energy brings out your best character qualities so others can see them too.

ONCE YOU CAN DO
THE THINGS
YOU TRULY WANT TO,
LIFE'S POSSIBILITIES
BECOME ENDLESS.

Don't listen to people who say it's a bad thing to want to be the centre of attention; MCE is about being the centre of *your* attention, and who isn't worthy of that? Your life is your book and you can write it however you like. Do you think Elle Woods let people's perceptions of her stop her from applying to Harvard? No. She worked hard and got in despite people thinking she was an airhead.

Prioritising yourself isn't always easy. There will be times when you doubt yourself and that's OK. Working on yourself is a journey and there will be some moments when you'll want to stop and get off the self-development train. But the work you put into yourself will be worth it and the person you become will thank you for it.

WHO DO *YOU* WANT TO BE?

We all have an image of who we'd like to be, and chances are you're already that person – you just don't know it yet.

MCE is all about bringing out your best qualities and accepting the ones you're not quite so keen on.

In essence, it's about creating a balance between accepting your flaws (because we all have them – we wouldn't be human if we didn't) and embracing all the things you love about yourself more than ever.

Why not try writing down all the things you like about yourself? It could be as little as liking how you organise your wardrobe or as big as liking how vulnerable you can be. Whatever it is, write it down. This list is a reminder of your greatness, so keep it somewhere you can regularly see it. Perhaps on your bathroom mirror.

Think about what steps you could take to make these likes into loves. Perhaps you'd like to take your organisational skills out of the wardrobe. What steps will make you love this about yourself? Focusing on turning likes into loves is a simple way to set your goals without being hard on yourself. You're brilliant just the way you are but it's OK to want to keep growing.

Main character energy isn't about bullying yourself into being a better person, it's about loving yourself into one.

WHO'S YOUR INSPIRATION?

While being your authentic self is super-important, there's nothing wrong with having a few role models who are living life in a way you want to.

Look at the likes of Lizzo, who lives, breathes and – quite frankly – *wears* self-love. Have you ever watched a Lizzo video and not smiled? Of course not.

She may be braver with her fashion choices than most people but there's nothing she can't get away with wearing because she's confident in who she is and is proud of how she looks.

Maybe bookish Eloise Bridgerton is more on your wavelength? While some of the other *Bridgerton* characters follow the rules by bowing and fawning in all the right places, she prefers concentrating on her studies and refuses to be anything other than who she is – incredibly smart and 100% herself. Going to lavish events in garish gowns and thirst-trapping just isn't her thing, and she's completely OK with that.

Then there are those people who have got that something you can't quite put your finger on. Take Timothée Chalamet, for example. Yeah, you could sharpen pencils on his cheekbones and one smile from him could have you swooning, but he's the kind of person you would know had walked into a room even if you were standing with your back to him. If you could bottle what he's got, we'd all order crates of the stuff.

Your role models don't have to be famous, either. You may work with them or learn alongside them. It could be a parent or another relative, or someone you know who does an incredible job that you would love to do one day, whether they're a nurse, an astronaut or a teacher. What character traits do they have that you admire and would like to emulate? What do you think makes them stand out? Make a note of them on your phone or get it down on paper, because we've got some life-enhancing exercises coming up later in the book.

BUT REMEMBER ... THEY'RE NOT YOU

Inspirations are just that – inspirations. No one is saying for a moment that you need to morph into someone else, because that would be a tragedy. The things that make you different from other people could be the best things about you; you just don't know it yet.

Uniqueness is a gift, and we are all different in wonderful ways. You do not need to change who you are because you're not good enough (you are more than good enough). It's about making subtle changes to make you feel like dynamite.

YOU DESERVE THE VERY BEST

Picture this: you're writing a movie about your life. How would you want that film to play out? In the best way possible, right? You'd have the perfect career, partner, friendships, home and clothes – plus an adorable pet. And, most importantly, you'd have inner peace and whole lot of love and support around you.

What would make you truly happy? If you're not completely sure, start thinking about it. Hard. You need to know what you want for yourself before you start planning how you're going to get it. Once you're clear, you can start aiming for the stars and manifesting that reality. More on this later.

Another great way to figure out your goals is to get to know yourself exactly as you are right now:

Think about how you would describe yourself if someone asked you what you were like. Draw a spider diagram of all the words you'd use. If you're stuck, ask your friends and family. They know you best and can help you identify your strengths and weaknesses.

Create two columns to list your likes and dislikes. This is completely based on you, not about what people on social media like or what you're supposed to think is cool. Really dig deep and jot down the things that bring you joy (maybe it's music and cooking) and the things that don't (maybe you're not keen on being in big groups or hate the taste of broccoli).

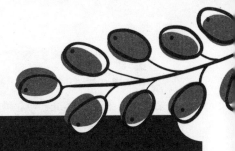

If there are things you love doing, why not do more of them? What's to stop you?

Think about something that makes you feel proud. An award you've won? A skill you've learned? Something or someone you stood up for? What makes you feel warm inside when you remember it? Think back to those moments one by one and let yourself feel the pride you felt at the time. Store that feeling in your mental locker and go back to it whenever you feel a bit flat.

What would you do if you had no fear of failure? Would you plan to travel the world on your own? Open an animal sanctuary? Become a high-powered businessperson? It doesn't have to be something that you plan to do for certain; it's about dreaming big. Imagine how it would feel to be there and who you would be with. Really experience it in your head. Just doing that will raise your energy and make you feel more excited about the future.

If you could only keep five things that you own, what would they be? Whether it's old photos your parents keep, your phone, your favourite jumper or your journal, what you choose will help you become clear on what really matters to you.

What are you passionate about? Is it helping the environment, ending homelessness, promoting feminism, supporting animal welfare or simply spreading love? Look online and see if there are any groups or local clubs you can join to indulge that interest, or create a passion board with pictures of things you love and hang it up somewhere you can see it every day.

Finally, what soothes you? Maybe it's cuddling your dog and watching a film, or messaging your best mate for hours at a time. Think about the things that make you feel calm if you ever notice your anxiety rising. They can come in really handy if you're needing an uplift. Not every day is easy and you need to have those go-tos to make you feel better.

LISTEN UP – THIS BIT IS REALLY IMPORTANT!

Channelling MCE does not involve changing your entire personality and who you are as a person; it involves you getting to know yourself inside out. It requires you to push yourself a little when it feels right, but not so much that it hurts.

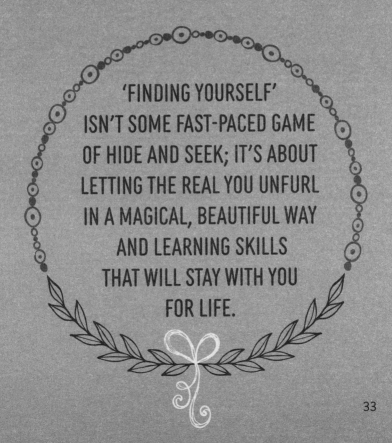

'FINDING YOURSELF'
ISN'T SOME FAST-PACED GAME
OF HIDE AND SEEK; IT'S ABOUT
LETTING THE REAL YOU UNFURL
IN A MAGICAL, BEAUTIFUL WAY
AND LEARNING SKILLS
THAT WILL STAY WITH YOU
FOR LIFE.

It's a bit like making a cake. If the base is rubbish, how can you build on it? You can add elaborate frosting, sparklers and sugar flowers, but if the cake itself is wet and wobbly, it's not going to be long before the whole thing collapses. You need to take the time to properly prepare and bake the cake. Then, when your base is fully cooked, you can begin decorating it.

You'll need to test yourself now and again to see if something is right for you or not. Like trying different icing on a cake. Otherwise, how will you know?

BUT ULTIMATELY, MCE
IS ABOUT BECOMING SO
COMFORTABLE WITH THE
PERSON YOU ALREADY ARE,
YOU NATURALLY RADIATE
CONFIDENCE AND
POSITIVITY.

You'll know when you've got there because you'll no longer feel the need to impress other people, and that is *incredibly* freeing. You won't constantly be questioning yourself because you'll know the answers. You won't need validation from others because you'll already know you rock. You'll wake up knowing what you want from your day/week/month/year/life. You'll feel truly yourself.

BAD DAYS ARE NORMAL

While some days you may wake up feeling like you could take on the world, other days you may feel more fragile and find yourself contemplating the meaning of life (which can take some time). That is what being human is all about.

No one leaps out of bed singing and dancing each morning. In fact, some days you may wake up and wonder how you're going to get through the day. Maybe you slept badly because you've got things on your mind or you have a hard day ahead of you and just know you're in for a tough one.

Bad days are a fact of life. An annoying one, but they cannot be avoided. Sometimes we have challenges

or upsetting things going on that we just have to get through. It's OK to stumble a little here and there, and the best thing you can do on those days is to be as kind to yourself as possible.

Don't berate yourself because your brain got scrambled and you forgot what you wanted to order in the coffee shop. Give yourself an internal hug and let inner you know that it's OK.

MCE is about praising yourself for the things you can do, not giving yourself a hard time for the things you can't – especially when you're trying to exist on three hours' sleep and all you want to do is curl up on the nearest sofa.

You might have as many hours in a day as Beyoncé, but that doesn't mean that you both don't find them hard sometimes.

Getting to the heart of who you are can feel painful at times too. You can experience sadness, release and regret. You may need to be patient because there are no shortcuts to changing

some things. But patience is just another talent you can add to your ever-growing list of genius qualities.

On the flip side, you're going to find out things about yourself you didn't even know existed. When you dig deep, you discover assets you didn't even know were assets.

If you feel like you've had a bad day, reflect on it and look for the little things that went *right*. Create a list in your head of the smallest things – like eating your favourite cake or seeing your best friend. That will lift you up a little and make you realise it wasn't *all* terrible. And tomorrow is another day you can make brilliant.

Simple ideas to get you started on your MCE journey

Set yourself a daily goal, whether it's being on time or deleting old WhatsApp messages. An easy goal is still a goal.

Think back to the last time you laughed.
Where were you?
What made you laugh?
Who were you with?
Does it still make you laugh?

Try one new thing today! Yeah, yeah, this one is beyond obvious, but stepping out of your comfort zone can give you a buzz and send your self-esteem skyrocketing. Start small. Maybe put on cobalt blue nail varnish instead of navy for a change?

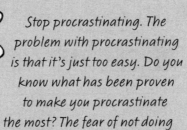

Stop procrastinating. The problem with procrastinating is that it's just too easy. Do you know what has been proven to make you procrastinate the most? The fear of not doing something right or achieving perfection (which we already know doesn't exist). Set a timer for twenty minutes and use that time to focus on one task. As soon as the timer goes off you can take a break, but you have to use those twenty minutes as solid concentration time.

FACT TIME:
DID YOU KNOW THAT WE'RE ONLY EVER BORN WITH TWO FEARS? LOUD NOISES AND FALLING.

Everything else, we learn as we grow up. If you have fears about not being good enough, they're limiting thoughts that might have wheedled their way into your head via a school bully or an overzealous sibling, and they can be challenged.

If change feels overwhelming, just start small. No one is expecting you to go to bed with insecurities and wake up with the confidence of Dua Lipa. But if you *keep* putting off trying to change the things you want to, you'll never get there.

Bad habits can come from our fears. It's time to work on banishing them. Not all at once, of course. Start small. If you can't stop biting your nails, try stopping for five minutes one day. The next day increase it to ten, and the next day fifteen. You get the picture . . . and if you find yourself back at square one? Try again.

Stop thinking of things as a disaster and see them as minor setbacks and opportunities to learn instead. It may sound weird, but if you can be grateful for them, it will change your whole perspective. Failure in general helps you grow and learn.

Think ahead and imagine how you'll feel once you kick that bad habit and use that to drive you on. The confidence boost will so be so worth it.

GO TO WAR WITH YOUR INNER CRITIC

Everyone – absolutely *everyone* – has an inner critic that's like a gremlin ready to pounce the moment you do something *wrong* and berate you for your failures.

Some people's gremlins are chilled and relaxed and only pop up every now and again to point out some small flaw, whilst other people have overly busy gremlins who are with them from dawn to dusk and spend as much time as possible pointing out every tiny little thing they do wrong. But the truth is, the gremlins are wrong.

BEATING YOURSELF
UP OVER POINTLESS THINGS
IS . . . WELL . . . POINTLESS.
YOU NEED TO FACE THAT
GREMLIN HEAD-ON AND LET
THEM KNOW WHO'S
IN CHARGE.

Take a few quiet minutes and think about it. Why would you criticise yourself when you have a choice? And you do! Letting your gremlin bully you is a form of self-sabotage, and main characters do not let other people – whether they're people or gremlins – allow them to feel bad about themselves.

One way to face your gremlin is to give it a name. If you can name your critic, it's easier to discredit them. Every time you hear them whispering in your ear, telling you someone is laughing at you or that you've said the wrong thing, simply say their name. This should make them quiet down.

The more you practise the easier it will get. Before long, it will be second nature and you won't even need to think about it. *You* are in charge of your thoughts, not your gremlin.

Our inner critics have developed as we've grown up. They're simply another unhelpful habit we've picked up without even realising it. But the great thing is that if something can be learned, it can also be *unlearned*.

CHAPTER 2

ROMANTICISE EVERY DAY

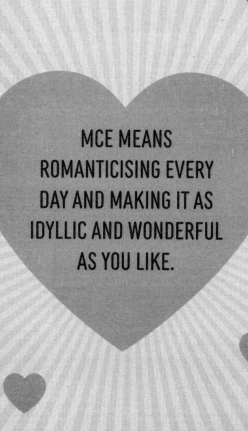

MCE MEANS
ROMANTICISING EVERY
DAY AND MAKING IT AS
IDYLLIC AND WONDERFUL
AS YOU LIKE.

MAKE EVERY DAY AMAZING – YOU DESERVE IT!

Planning the perfect day doesn't take hours of preparation – we can't all have Rory Gilmore levels of organisation – so start small. Make sure you have at least one thing you're excited about doing in the hours ahead, even if it is just reading a chapter of your favourite book or finishing off that podcast you've been saving for the perfect moment. Remember, any moment can be a perfect one if you make it one.

A great day is all about planning ahead, so keep a notebook and a pen by the side of your bed. Each night, just before you turn the light off, write down your goals for the following day. It can be one really important thing that you want to focus all of your attention on or several things that you're aiming towards. If you've got long-term goals, you can write them down each night, but always add at least one thing you know you can wake up and feel excited about. Make sure it's achievable and will bring you joy. No matter how big or small the goal is, you've set your intention for the new day and that's an excellent way to start.

SOUND THE ALARM

No one likes getting out of bed. The more duvet time the better. But setting your alarm ten minutes early will give you time to focus on yourself before the demands of everyday life begin. Maybe spend the extra time stretching and deep breathing to waken up and get yourself into a calm headspace. Think about the things you want to achieve that day and why

they're important to you. What order are you going to do them in? Which goal are you most excited to achieve? Taking the time to prepare yourself for your day makes it all the more likely that you'll achieve your goals. You're more focused and determined than you would be if you were rushing around with just enough time to get ready for the day.

Another surefire way to start your day off right – make your bed. Making your bed only takes seconds and is already a task ticked off your to-do list. Having a freshly made bed will, firstly, stop you from climbing back into it and, secondly, spur you on to do more. It's OK that you'll mess it up again when you get into bed that night.

It may sound obvious and a bit basic, but this technique is used in the military every day. According to experts, doing this simple chore gives you a sense of pride and reminds your brain that little things matter. It serves as positive encouragement for keeping the rest of your bedroom tidy and even makes you feel calmer. When your environment is less cluttered and more streamlined, it can give you a sense of lightness and make your head feel less manic. It will also feel so nice when you get home later that day and your bed's all ready for you to slide back into.

GOOD MORNING!

Writing morning pages is a brilliant way to process the previous day, decode your dreams and clear your mind for the day ahead.

It's a super simple activity that's really similar to journaling, except rather than stopping to think about what you want to write, you let it flow out like a stream of consciousness and allow whatever thoughts you have to be committed to paper.

It's a freeing activity and you'll probably be surprised to find that it could spawn some of your most creative ideas. Sometimes when we look too hard for things, they become more deeply buried, but when you read over your brain dump and reflect on what you said, you'll be surprised at the wisdom staring back at you.

If you fancy getting creative with your hands instead, do some drawing or doodling. Channel your inner Banksy and let your

imagination run wild. When you use your hands in a creative way, it exercises different parts of your brain, which helps you to regain energy and feel joy. You may even discover hidden talents, which will increase your confidence.

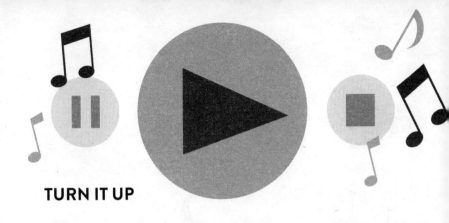

TURN IT UP

It goes without saying that no MCE day is complete without the right playlist. Inspiration for yours can come from anywhere – whether you're feeling ready to take on the day with *The Guardians of the Galaxy's* epic soundtrack or need to feel what you want to feel with Lady Gaga and Bradley Cooper's version of 'Shallow' on repeat.

Playlists can completely alter your mood, giving you the confidence to strut (if you're so inclined) out of the house ready to take on the day. No one else can hear what you're listening to when you have your headphones on, so why not stream a girl power playlist or listen to some happy hits.

Playlists are also perfect for when you just need to let yourself feel all the feelings. This is completely OK and, in fact, very healthy. If you have a hard day, come home and turn up the sad songs. Give yourself space to feel and breathe. Then, when you've let yourself feel all the sadness, anguish and frustration you needed to feel, switch over to some of your favourite upbeat songs and cheer yourself up again. The whole day isn't a write-off just because you've spent some time feeling low. The rest of the day is yours to enjoy.

THE SMALL BUT MIGHTY MOMENTS

Channelling your main character energy is not about the big moments. It's not all about the fairy-tale endings of movies where the protagonist is crowned prom queen or gets that big promotion at work. The little things are just as important. Cuddling a kitten or playing with other animals can release a huge burst of serotonin in your brain, keeping you smiling for hours. Even buying yourself a small treat can give you a rush of adrenaline. Reminding yourself to acknowledge the small moments of joy in your day will instantly increase your energy. It doesn't have to cost a penny either. It could be calling a friend, taking a long bath, lying in your bed listening to a podcast or spotting a new flower growing in the garden. All of these things are free, and taking the time to look for them will instantly brighten your mood for the day.

HOW TO DISCOVER NEW THINGS THAT BRING YOU JOY

The world is a big old place and there is so much out there still to be discovered. Some things that you don't even know about yet are going to light your heart up. Or you'll rediscover old things you used to love to do and have forgotten about over the years. Life should be filled with as much happiness as possible and one of the best ways to achieve this is to find the things that bring you joy. Here are a few things you could try:

Take a class – Have you been desperate to try out a new hobby but feeling too nervous? Do it! Sign up for that art, pottery or cooking class. Not every pottery class is a re-enactment of Ghost! Quite often you can find taster classes for free or half price. They're a great way to try the hobby out before you commit.

Puzzles – This one may be a little old school but is a classic for a reason. Doing jigsaws or mind puzzles can be ridiculously relaxing, and they're also super good for your brain. You switch off the emotional part of your brain whilst you concentrate on puzzles, so you can truly absorb yourself in them. Plus, you'll feel really clever when you complete the puzzle.

Music – You are never too old to learn an instrument. Even if you just buy a recorder and learn 'Frère Jacques', you're learning a new skill. If Amanda Bynes can learn to play football for *She's the Man*, you can try and new hobbie!

Being in nature – One for the cottagecore queens. Bird watching, forest bathing, cold water swimming – all fantastic hobbies for the nature lover in you and a great way to ground yourself when life feels overwhelming.

Cake decorating – When you don't have time to actually bake a cake, let your creativity flow by decorating one. Whether you go with a simple buttercream icing or an elaborate masterpiece, you'll definitely enjoy this one. Decorate your cake and eat it.

JUST SAY YES!

Whether or not you take up forest bathing or cake decorating, the lesson is to say yes! Take a leap of faith and try something new. Even if it doesn't lead to a lifelong hobby, it's a fun way to discover something new about yourself and to find out what you don't want to do with your time. You have amazing hidden strengths and talents you don't even know about yet. But you'll only find out what they are by saying yes more often when opportunities come your way. If something turns out not to be for you? Great, at least you'll know! It would be worse to always wonder than to know for sure.

Who knows what saying yes could lead to? That simple three-letter word could change the course of your life for ever. If you're tempted to say no because you're worried about not knowing how to do something, learn as you go. Sometimes it's the only way.

Saying yes is also empowering. It's telling yourself you're willing to go out of your comfort zone even if it means you fail. Failure is not a reflection on who you are as a person but the way in which life likes to teach us lessons. While it may sting at the time, you will look back on that experience with enormous affection for what it taught you. After you say yes to something challenging once, you'll do it again because it will increase your confidence, open up new worlds of possibility and allow you to meet new people. It just takes that one small word and the world gets a little bit bigger for you. YES!

HOW TO BECOME A #COTTAGECOREQUEEN

We live in a fast-paced world. Even if you live in the countryside, there's no getting away from technology, news, messages, phone calls and our internal monologues. It's no wonder the cottagecore aesthetic has become so popular. Who doesn't dream of swinging gently in a homemade hammock in the middle of a beautiful blossoming garden, wearing cute floral fits and picking wildflowers to display in their kitchen windows? It's idyllic for a reason.

If you're not familiar with the cottagecore trend – also sometimes known as countrycore or farmcore – it centres on getting back to nature and slow living. Think baking bread, growing vegetables or sewing your own clothes. It's straight out of a Jane Austen movie with the plucky heroine running through a lavender field wearing a romantic flowing dress and being completely caught up in the joy of the moment.

Cottagecore is all about taking time to enjoy the everyday

and sometimes even the mundaneness of life. Although the style might not be what you want to wear, there's a lot to learn from the trend. The beauty of it is that you can make your interpretation of cottagecore anything you want it to be. As long as you're living slowly – that is to say, being mindful of your actions. It could be anything from taking the time to prepare and enjoy your meals without sitting in front of the TV to going on a long walk just because it's sunny. We can't all up sticks and move to the middle of nowhere to escape from everyday life but we can take the time to live in the moment.

HOW TO COUNTRIFY YOUR BEDROOM

One way to indulge in your cottagecore fantasies and start living mindfully is by adopting the aesthetic. You can put your own spin on any of these recommendations, but just by taking the time to think about every piece you put in your space, you're already practising slow living.

Cosy bedding – An absolute essential when creating your dream bedroom. Think blankets, quilts, throws and cushions in pale, earthy and vintage prints. You want to make it look and feel as snug as possible, as if your problems will melt away the minute you climb inside.

Plants – Another cottagecore essential. Part of the appeal is to bring the outside in and be at one with nature, and plants are the easiest way to do that. They are also proven to reduce anxiety, and certain plants like peace lilies help to clean and filter air.

Flowers – If you struggle to keep plants alive, fear not – flowers can do the trick just the same. Whether you buy real ones or not, they can add colour to your space and are an instant mood booster. Why not try sticking pieces of Blu Tack on the stems and arrange them in rows to make it look like they're growing up the wall.

The little details – No room is complete without candles. Pick smells that calm you or remind you of fond memories, or smells you just can't get enough of. Dream catchers, dried flowers and photos of family and friends all make your space feel relaxing too. You could also try filling a mason jar with affirmations or notes friends have given you for instant pick-me-ups when you're feeling down.

Light – If you're not lucky enough to have lots of natural light in your space, then invest in some warm, soft lighting. Fairy lights and bedside lamps can give your space that homely feel. Strategically placing mirrors opposite windows will also help any natural light to bounce around the room and give the illusion of a brighter space. An instance mood booster!

A safe space – Create a reading nook where you can lose yourself in a book – a cottagecore fan would probably read a romance or historical novel. It doesn't need to cost anything. You just need a comfy chair or a few floor cushions, a soft blanket and a reading light with a low wattage bulb (to give a mellow, natural glow). This will make the perfect cosy spot.

THE LOOK

You can't romanticise your life without dressing the part. Cottagecore looks are the perfect blend between romantic and rugged, so there's something for everyone looking to channel their MCE. You can tailor any of these suggestions to your own aesthetic. You don't have to go completely Carrie Bradshaw and wear a newspaper for a dress. As long as you're dressing how you want to, it doesn't matter what anyone else may think – it's all about you.

Patterns – Florals, stripes and gingham are central to the cottagecore aesthetic. Pair them with seaside pastels, muted tones and freshly washed whites and you've got the style down to a tee.

Oversized is the new undersized – Jumpers and cardigans that look a couple of sizes too big, with extra-long arms that cover your hands, and made from cotton, wool or yarn are perfect for chilly autumn walks or curling up with a book.

Timeless pieces – From Victorian aprons and Edwardian puff-sleeved blouses to twenties floor-length skirts, anything goes. Feel free to layer and wear different patterns even if they clash. They just add to the feel.

Footwear to frolic in – Anything from cutesy Mary Janes and ballet pumps to Dr. Martens are acceptable. Pair that floral dress with a pair of work boots.

Hold your head high – Your hair can be whatever it wants to be, whether it's natural, long, tied up in loose buns or plaited in braids. Whatever makes you feel good. The same goes for make-up too. With or without it, the cottagecore look is definitely minimal, so there's no need to spend a lot of time on it.

OUTSIDE IS THE NEW INSIDE

Immersing yourself in cottagecore means immersing yourself in nature, which also happens to be one of the best things you can do for your mental wellbeing. Taking time away from your phone (the average person in the UK spends around four hours a day on their phone) allows you to take in the world around you, and the more you do it the less you care about your social media feed or the group WhatsApp chain.

You don't have to do away with your phone completely and start climbing Mount Everest, but spending even half an hour a day outside will do wonders for your mood, lower your stress levels and improve your attention span. Even if you're just stopping to notice flowers as you walk past them in your local park, you'll feel an uplift in your soul.

Just the sound of nature can be beneficial, so if you're too busy in your book nook to embrace the outside world, throw open your door and listen to the birds singing or the sound of the wind blowing the leaves off the trees. All those gentle outside sounds we take for granted have a calming impact on our inner world.

CHAPTER 3

WORKING ON YOURSELF

SET YOUR GOALS

Social media is overflowing with people talking about manifesting/scripting/wish-making. The idea is that all we need to do is believe that we're capable of getting what we want and then it will happen. Celebs love it, social media influencers stand by it and it became one of the main quarantine trends during COVID times (as well as baking banana bread).

Not sure what you want to manifest just yet? It can be tricky, but one thing you can do to help set your goals is to make a vision board. A vision board will help you get aligned with your goals, values and intentions and send a message out to the universe about what you'd like to change and receive in your life. It's a creative way to help you work out what you want, on both a conscious *and* a subconscious level. It allows you to delve into your inner world and ask yourself questions without the distraction of outside influences.

It can also help you to focus on the future. It's like drawing the universe a map of where you want to be in one, three or five years' time and deciding what happiness looks like to you at each of those points. Although you might not always be exactly where you'd hoped to be (the universe often plays tricks on you like that), you're on this journey for a reason and every setback is a lesson. That's the magic of vision boards – there's a pleasing element of surprise so you never know what's around the corner.

If you find that you're the sort of person who needs a visual reminder of your goals, then this chapter is for you. Whether you want to proudly display your vision board or keep it hidden for your eyes only, creating a physical vision board is a great way of reminding yourself of your goals every day and continuing to work towards them. Try following these steps below for making your board:

Step 1) Read through old journals or goal lists and think about which goals still resonate with you.

Step 2) Do a brain dump of everything you would like to manifest. The sky is the limit and anything and everything is allowed!

Step 3) Dig out some old magazines or look online for any images that inspire you – pictures and words – and align with your dreams and goals. Print and cut them out.

Step 4) Arrange the pictures, notes and words on the vision board and work out how you would like it to look before you start gluing. That way, you can change things around if it doesn't feel quite right.

Step 5) Once you're happy with the overall look, it's commitment time. Start sticking and securing things in place. It doesn't matter if anything overlaps, as long as the things that are important to you are clear to see.

Step 6) Write encouraging messages to yourself around your goals. These are reminders of why you're manifesting these goals and that they are achievable.

Step 7) Embellish! Let your inner child run wild with all the glitter, rainbow gel pens and stickers you want. As long as it looks exciting to you, that's all that matters.

Step 8) Find the perfect place for your vision board to live. Ideally somewhere you'll see it every day. You can also take a photo of it and make it your wallpaper on your phone so it's always there to refer to.

NOW IT'S TIME TO LET THE UNIVERSE DO ITS THING.

OUT WITH THE OLD

The best way to start living your new main character life is to let go of the old one. This doesn't mean buying a whole new wardrobe or moving to a new country – this isn't the beginning of a Hallmark movie. It's simply about taking the time to let go of the things in your life that don't serve a purpose any more.

Take the advice of expert organiser Marie Kondo and as you sort through your things, ask yourself, 'Does it bring me joy?' If it doesn't, then it no longer has a place in your life and you can either donate it, sell it, swap it or repurpose it.

Sorting – The best place to start is your wardrobe, since your clothes are the things you interact with most in your home. Go through your wardrobe and make two piles: one of the things you genuinely love and will wear again and one with things you no longer like or you only bought because you thought you should.

Repurpose – Don't forget you can alter your clothes to give them a new lease of life or make your own cushion covers out of an old duvet cover. Even if you don't have the sewing skills to hem a new suit, there are lots of quick fixes for upcycling your old things.

Getting swapping – Your trash could be your friends' treasure. Invite your friends over for a swap party and see what old item of theirs would look perfect in your space.

Sell, sell, sell – With the pile you no longer want to keep, decide which pieces are in good enough condition to sell. You can list them online or sell them to second-hand stores – then use the cash to buy items that do bring you joy and align with your goals.

Donate – Everything else can be donated to charity shops or clothing recycling centres. Clothes and household goods that aren't in good enough condition to be resold in a charity shop can still make them money from recycling, so offer them up there first before heading to the recycling centre.

SUPERSTAR SKIN

We should all be comfortable with the skin we're in, but when it comes to our facial skincare, that means taking good care of it so we can exude face-confidence. Part of being your authentic self is appreciating how much our skin does for us. In a literal sense, our skin is our first barrier to illness, it helps us to stay hydrated and it regulates our temperature to keep us comfortable. It's pretty miraculous, and that puts the pimples or blemishes that we sometimes get into perspective.

OUR SKIN IS IMPORTANT, SO WE NEED TO LOOK AFTER IT!

Some easy skincare tips experts swear by are:

Routine is key – Find a regime that works and stick to it. There are some brilliant websites and apps that will analyse your skin and suggest the best products for your age/skin type.

Keep it simple – You don't need fancy products or a ten-step routine to look after your skin. Try a couple of basic products with simple ingredients until you find what works for you. Using a cleanser and a moisturiser is a good place to start.

TikTok made me buy it – Don't use a product just because everyone else on TikTok is. Like us, our skin is unique, and just because someone is raving about a serum revitalising their skin it doesn't mean it's going to do the same for yours.

Double cleanse – Once isn't enough! Skin experts recommended cleansing your skin once in the morning but doing the double at night so you can be sure you've wiped away any trace of foundation, highlighter or mascara. Make sure you don't rush because it can take a while for your make-up to loosen up.

Detox – Using a face mask once a week can do everything from drawing out impurities to hydrating and toning. Again, find what works for your skin. Applying face masks once or twice a week is enough to help you skin stay calm.

Wear SPF every day – Sun cream isn't just for holidays. Even when it's overcast and miserable out, the winter sun still breaks through the clouds and can cause damage to your skin, no matter your skin type. UV rays are harmful any time of year, not just when the sun is at its brightest, so apply SPF every morning to protect your skin. Mineral-based SPFs are highly recommended because they are light, allow your skin to breathe and are also ocean-friendly.

CHANNELLING MAJOR MAIN CHARACTER HAIR ENERGY

Just like clothes and make-up, hair is individual to us all. A pixie cut may look cool on an influencer or celeb, but it doesn't mean you have to go for the chop.

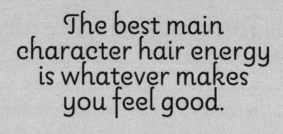

The best main character hair energy is whatever makes you feel good.

Start small by building a regular hair care routine – find products that help your hair. Like skincare, keeping it simple is best, but your hairdresser can help you find the right routine.

Experiment with different styles like bubble braids, T-shirt roll curls, Bantu knots, messy buns and afro puffs. Whatever your hair type, there are fun hairstyles out there for you.

DIY NAILS TO SUIT YOUR STYLE

Another way to help you feel your best as you put yourself first is to take care of the little things. Manicures and pedicures can be super expensive, so why not try these at-home tips to do on yourself or with a friend.

The perfect DIY manicure (also applies to pedicures):

1.

Apply nail polish remover to clean your nails and remove any last traces of old nail.

2.

File and buff your nails using a nail buffer. You can usually pick up buffers in pound shops.

3.

Exfoliate your hands. You can use any face or body exfoliator to do this Simply wet the skin and slowly massage the exfoliator in circles. Then wash off.

4.

Moisturise your hands with a cream or oil.

5.

Apply a base coat to your nails and allow it to dry for two minutes. This will help to keep your polish in place.

6.

Apply your first colour coat to your nails, making sure you go all the way up to the cuticles and sides. You can clean up any overlaps later.

7.

Wait two minutes and apply your second coat. Very light or sheer colours may need a third coat – if so, simply repeat.

8.

Once you know the polish is totally dry, grab a nail art pen and get creative. Draw whatever you like on your nails, from flowers to peace signs to Halloween pumpkins. Whatever you fancy!

9.

Once your designs are a hundred per cent dry, apply a top coat and give yourself a nice five minutes to chill while it sets.

10.

If you've got any uneven edges, pop a cotton bud in some polish remover and very carefully trace around the sides of your nails to remove any excess polish.

TA-DA!
YOU'RE GOOD TO GO.

THIS IS ALL FOR YOU

Now that you've spent time setting your goals and working on the physical changes you want for yourself, it's time to reflect on how your main character journey is going. You *look* fabulous, but it's important that you *feel* that way too. You're on this journey for no one but yourself and it's important not to forget that. You might have changed your hairstyle or restyled your space, but at your core you're still the brilliant and interesting person who started reading this book. Hopefully you now feel more confident about that person and want to share more of them with the world.

TRY TO BE THE PERSON YOU REALLY ARE DEEP DOWN AND ALWAYS WANTED TO BE. IF YOU CHOOSE TO CHANGE ANYTHING ABOUT YOURSELF, IT SHOULD ALWAYS BE ON YOUR TERMS. YOU ARE AND ALWAYS WILL BE THE MAIN CHARACTER, NO MATTER WHAT YOU'RE WEARING. DON'T LET YOURSELF FORGET THAT.

CHAPTER 4

YOUR SUPPORTING
CAST

SUPPORTING CHARACTERS

Friends are a massively important part of all our lives and true friends are invaluable. They support, love and lift us up, and when you find people you can talk to about anything, any time, there's nothing quite like it. When you find your tribe, you feel like you're a part of something, and that's super special.

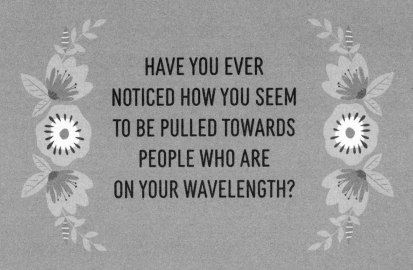

HAVE YOU EVER NOTICED HOW YOU SEEM TO BE PULLED TOWARDS PEOPLE WHO ARE ON YOUR WAVELENGTH?

It's like there's an invisible forcefield between you that is sending out signals saying 'we should be mates'.

Equally, while you might not necessarily *dislike* someone, you won't always get on with everyone. You'll usually know pretty quickly whether someone you meet is going be a person you say hi to now and again or someone you'll be lifelong friends with.

As you continue your main character journey, it's important to recognise the importance of the cast of supporting characters around you. Without their influence you wouldn't be the person you are today and the person you want to be is likely a reflection of many of them.

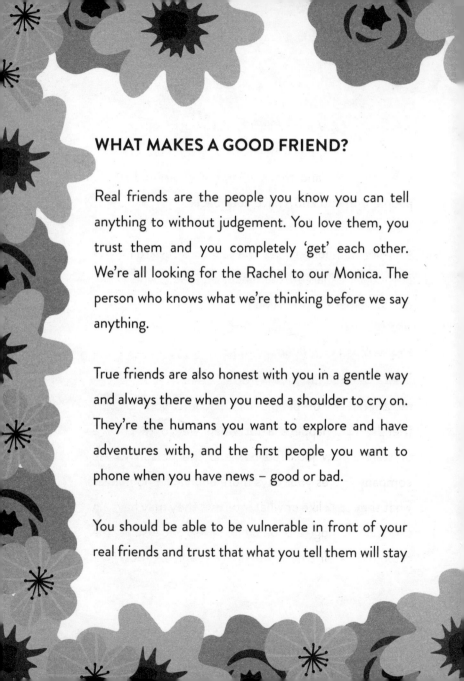

WHAT MAKES A GOOD FRIEND?

Real friends are the people you know you can tell anything to without judgement. You love them, you trust them and you completely 'get' each other. We're all looking for the Rachel to our Monica. The person who knows what we're thinking before we say anything.

True friends are also honest with you in a gentle way and always there when you need a shoulder to cry on. They're the humans you want to explore and have adventures with, and the first people you want to phone when you have news – good or bad.

You should be able to be vulnerable in front of your real friends and trust that what you tell them will stay between you. Vulnerability is a strength and not a weakness, but it needs to be expressed in the right way, and that's when you're around the people who you know have your back.

Allowing someone to see the real us is rewarding and a wonderful shared experience, especially when they can be vulnerable with you too.

Friendship doesn't mean you have to like all the same things, either. Sometimes opposites attract and the most unlikely of people can become your closest friends. This happens a lot when we go to college or start a new job. You befriend the person whose company makes your days more enjoyable, no matter what they look like or what interests they may have. In short, don't judge a book by its cover, because people often hide their true self behind a tough exterior.

What about when it comes to being a good friend yourself? See above! Think about the qualities you would like in a friend and then be that person to *your* friends. These could include:

Always having their back

Checking in on them if you think they're feeling down

Making space and time for them in your life

Being a person they can trust and a sympathetic ear

Follow your own rules and treat people how you want to be treated, and you can't go wrong.

Friendships can be magical and should always – *always* – enhance your life, not detract from it. It's OK to outgrow friends or recognise when a friendship isn't working and step away. You are worthy of feeling good at all times and you shouldn't continue friendships with people who don't let you feel that way.

THE TRIALS AND TRIBULATIONS OF FRENEMIES

It's normal to want to be liked. It makes us feel warm inside and reassured that we are interesting people and enjoyable company. It makes us want to be nice to other people too. But now and again we befriend people who may not have our best interests at heart and suddenly we wish that they didn't like us.

Frenemies could be those 'friends' you've known since day one or someone you met last month, but they're equally easy to spot. Sometimes they become the Dwight Schrute to our Jim Halpert, a frenemy we learn to love. They're the kind of people who will gaslight you, put you down in front of other people, drop you if someone else comes along, point out when you do things wrong and talk about you behind your back. It's a sad fact that hurt people hurt people. If someone is trying to hurt you, it's probably because they're hurting inside themselves, but that doesn't make it OK.

Most of us are people-pleasers and that makes it really hard to shake those people who make us feel bad about ourselves, because we feel guilty. You don't want to seem like the bad guy by pulling away, but equally, why should someone be allowed to undo all the amazing work you're doing on yourself by undermining you?

People pleasing and wanting to be liked keeps us suppressed and gives other people power over us. Sometimes we even change to fit in with how they want us to be, and that is the complete *opposite* of MCE. If you become what someone else wants you to be, you could easily end up being everything to everyone else and nothing to yourself.

There is absolutely no shame in letting friendships go if they are no longer working for you. It doesn't make you a bad person and you're not the one in the wrong. Some people are in our lives for a reason and some just a season. Not all friendships are going to be lifelong unions. If you think the friendship is worth saving, there's no harm in having a serious one-on-one to see if things can be resolved. But if the other person gets defensive and tries to put it back on you? They are not worth your energy.

THINK OF IT LIKE THIS: IF YOU RELEASE SOMEONE FROM YOUR LIFE BECAUSE THEY'RE DOING YOU MORE HARM THAN GOOD, YOU'RE MAKING SPACE FOR SOMEONE WHO APPRECIATES YOUR BRILLIANCE TO COME ALONG AND TAKE THEIR PLACE.

WHY IT'S OK NOT TO LIKE EVERYONE (AND VICE VERSA)

There are over eight billion people in the world, all with different likes and dislikes and thoughts and feelings. Humans are complex, to say the least. It would be weird if we *all* liked each other. It's natural to want to be liked by everyone but that's not a healthy expectation to put on ourselves. In the same way energy can draw people together, it can also repel people. If something is repelling you away from someone else, let it. There's a reason this is happening.

It's a tricky thing to navigate, but it is impossible to be friends with everyone you meet. Can you imagine how exhausting that would be? And how much time you'd have to dedicate to socialising? It doesn't mean you have to go around not liking people; you can simply feel indifferent. Being resentful or angry is exhausting, so it's much easier to accept that you won't be crafting quilts together anytime soon and move on.

Trying to validate yourself according to how many people like you is equally exhausting. Other people's opinions of you are none of your business. If you can free yourself from the shackles of caring what other people think, you can truly begin to put yourself first. The only opinions that should matter are those of the people you love and care about the most, and those people will never pull you down.

FALLOUT FAILS

Another thing we have to accept as a normal part of life and friendships is fallouts. They're going to happen every now and again – that's inevitable – but the worst thing you can do is catastrophise. A small argument doesn't mean your friendship with someone is over and done with. It's often easier and more common to fall out with people you're closest to because you have formed a sibling-type relationship where you forget to filter what you say. It can be easy to take best friends for granted if you've known each other for a long time because you think it will still be OK if you cross a line.

If you do bicker with a mate, before you step into victim mode, take a step back and look at your part in it. Did you overstep the mark? Did you say something hurtful without realising it? Was a joke taken the wrong way? If you think your friend was in the wrong, give them a chance to apologise, but don't let it all linger for too long. Real, solid friendships are special, so there has to be a bit of wiggle room for both sides to accept the fallout and move on.

WHY BEING POPULAR CAN BE OVERRATED

Anyone can *seem* like they've got tons of friends. People can rack up millions of likes on social media for saying 'funny' or mean things about other people. From a distance, that can seem like they're on a popularity pedestal. But look a bit closer and it just means people who like mean people like them.

Being 'liked' and being 'popular' are poles apart. Chances are you know a person you think has got everything when it comes to popularity. Everyone thinks they've got a super-supportive friendship group because everyone is always going on about how amazing they are. For all you know, they could feel the exact opposite. They may have loads of social media friends but very few real friends and feel incredibly lonely. It is not a case of the bigger the friendship circle the better someone is. It's better to have a couple of close friends then twenty people who hardly know you.

FINDING YOUR TRIBE

As cliché as it is, once you find your real friends you have a family for life. Like on those nature documentaries, your tribe will have your back when the carnivores attack – in this case, when life gets hard. Your tribe doesn't always look how you expect it to, and not having any expectations is the key.

You may have met your closest friends way back in nursery and still be going strong, or you may still be looking for a circle of mates who will become your support network. Like romantic relationships, finding your community happens at different times for different people.

You are one hundred per cent more likely to find people you'll be long-term friends with if you're being your authentic self. There's no point in pretending to be someone just to fit in with a popular group, because you'll either get sick of putting on a show or you'll be found out. When you're being you, you'll invite the right people in without even having to do anything. You'll also meet people with similar interests to you, as if you're being your authentic self, you'll be doing the activities you love and this is a great way to make friends, especially after you leave education and new people aren't introduced to you so frequently.

HOW TO BE HAPPY BEING SINGLE

At the heart of putting yourself first is recognising that the most important relationship you will ever have is with yourself. It's that straightforward. People will come in and out of your life, but the only person you can guarantee won't let you down or break your heart is yourself.

Being single isn't always easy, especially when it feels like all of your friends are loved up, even if only one is actually in a relationship! But it is always better to be single than in a relationship that isn't making you happy.

Being single can be the best thing to happen to you! Having time on your own gives you the chance to work out what you want from a relationship, and it also shows you how strong and independent you are. But best of all? If you can be happy on your own, it's concrete proof that you don't need anyone to make you feel good about yourself.

Going on dates can be loads of fun and having shared experiences with people you care about is priceless, but at times the best dates you can have are with yourself, creating memories for you and you alone.

Solo dating is very much a *thing*. Honouring yourself and doing what you love with no judgment from others is a really healthy way of putting yourself first. It will help you learn resilience and make you realise how good it feels to be comfortable in your own company. Whether you're in a relationship or not, solo dates are a great chance to try new things and push yourself out of your comfort zone. Why not try some of the solo date suggestions below.

Go for a coffee date with your favourite person (you). Throw in some cake too.

Take yourself to the cinema and buy a tub of popcorn that will take you the entire length of the film to finish.

Go for a walk in the park and listen to your favourite podcast.

Go to a museum and take in the art at your own pace.

Be a tourist in your town. Look up things to do where you live, whether it's taking a historical walk or visiting a local attraction.

Go to the theatre and see what you want without someone whispering in your ear asking what's going on!

Have a cosy home date. Pick your favourite movie, put on your comfy clothes and snuggle up with your favourite treats for the evening.

Go to the library and spend hours perusing sections you would never usually look at.

Cook yourself dinner. Try something new – and if it's terrible? There's always toast!

Go to an exercise class you've never tried before.

PUTTING YOURSELF FIRST WHEN FALLING IN LOVE

Before you meet the person of your dreams, you need to know what you want from a relationship. Give yourself some alone time (TV off, candles on) and write a really honest list of everything you would like from love. Even if you think it's a bit weird, put it down. There really could be someone else out there who loves 1940s French art house films.

If you're not clear on the kind of person you'd like to meet and how you'd like the relationship to play out, how are you going to know what energy you want to send out to the universe? It's true that we attract the kind of love we think we deserve, so it's time to start thinking of yourself highly so that your future partner thinks that too.

121

LOOK WHO'S HERE!

Let's fast forward (if you're single) or rewind (if you're not) and talk about boundaries. It's so easy to leap into a relationship with all kinds of expectations and get lost in the excitement of it all. But hold on! You've done all this work to become the main character you deserve to be and you cannot let someone come along and sweep it away from under you.

You should never have to change yourself to make someone happy or to fit in with what they want in a partner. You truly are perfect as you are, and your ideal partner will think that too.

Likewise, you should never date someone hoping that their personality or ambitions will change, because that's an unfair expectation. People are creatures of habit and although it's true that bad habits can be unlearned, the majority of the time, they won't be. Don't waste time dating someone with the expectation that they'll change because it's very unlikely they actually will.

The most important thing to look for in a relationship is balance. No one should have the upper hand, and ideally it should all flow naturally. Playing games is a waste of time, so don't even bother. A relationship isn't a competition to see who can hold out from saying 'I love you' the longest. If you want to say it, say it. If they don't say it back, maybe they're just not quite there yet. If they say it to you and you aren't quite there yet, don't fake it. It's important to go at a pace that is comfortable to you.

NOT YOUR FAULT

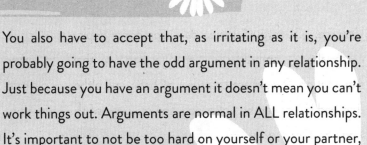

You also have to accept that, as irritating as it is, you're probably going to have the odd argument in any relationship. Just because you have an argument it doesn't mean you can't work things out. Arguments are normal in ALL relationships. It's important to not be too hard on yourself or your partner, if you have them. Instead, take the time to work through what you argued about, with a calm approach. This doesn't

have to be right after the argument (it's always good to have some time on your own to process it first) but it is important to talk through the issue rather than ignoring it.

If you're feeling worked up about it (which is likely), take some time to relax. Maybe do some deep breathing to calm down your nervous system or take a walk. It's important to get things into perspective, so don't rush to have your post-argument debrief until you've both completely calmed down.

Equally, if you keep bickering and the relationship no longer feels fun, it could be time to let

it go. If you're staying with someone just because you feel bad or you don't want to be on your own, you're robbing that person of the opportunity to meet someone else who doesn't mind that they eat tuna sandwiches and then try to kiss you. You're also stopping yourself from moving on and meeting someone who could light you up.

No matter what the situation, ignoring, ghosting or blocking is not acceptable. At least be respectful enough to let the other person know you're finished, even if you can't handle doing it face-to-face. Again, treat people how you would like to be treated.

EVERYONE GETS DUMPED SOMETIMES

There is no positive side to being dumped and there's no point trying to pretend there is. It sucks. Are you allowed to cry about it? Of course! Are you allowed to let it damage your self-esteem? No way! If this person doesn't want to be with you, then they are not the right person for you. One day you may even feel grateful to them for ending the relationship and helping you realise how much more you're worth.

MAIN COUPLE ENERGY

You and your partner have been together for a while and things are going well. You know it's right because you respect and like the way they are outside of the relationship as opposed to just being attracted to their appearance or how they are when you're alone together.

Now it's time for you to channel that main couple energy. Whether you're a Monica and Chandler, a Brittany and

Santana or a Mitch and Cam, we all have work to do on our relationships. Here are some top tips on how to support your co-star (because relationships are an ongoing project).

Work as a team – You're at your best when you're working together. Whether you're hosting an event together or planning a day out, communicate and work as a couple.

Work apart too – Strong couples don't rely on each other for everything. They give each other space to work on themselves or their own hobbies. This is crucial for maintaining each other's values and confidence. You don't need to be together 24/7.

Appreciate the little things – It's good to stop and smell the roses every now and again. Take the time to be grateful for the small gestures as well as the really big ones. A thank you for these goes a long way.

Support each other – Your significant other can't hang out this week because they're working on a big project? Send them an encouraging text or drop some snacks round. They'd do the same for you.

Be happy for each other – If one of you does well, the other should be their number one cheerleader. Think of your partner's success as your own success and celebrate it as such. It's OK if you feel a little bit jealous, but don't let that diminish your partners moment. Celebrate it!

CHAPTER 5

SELF-CARE

SELF-CARE FOR THE SOUL

Self-care is giving yourself and the world the best, happiest version of you, not the version that's left over after you've run around making sure everyone else is happy and looked after.

Self-care isn't selfish; it's quite the opposite. If you're giving too much of yourself away all the time, you're going to end up worn and run down, and then you won't be able to do anything for anyone, whether that's yourself or others. The key word to think about here? Boundaries.

We all want to be there for our friends and family and that's incredibly important, but at the end of the day, the only person you're *really* responsible for is yourself.

Boundaries protect your happiness and stop you from giving too much of yourself away. Be clear on how far you will go to help others before it becomes detrimental to you.

Are there times when you know you should say no and you don't? If so, it's time to get comfortable with using the word more often. You are not a pushover; you are discovering yourself through your individual plotline. If someone is getting in the way or trying to sabotage your journey, they've got to go.

If you surround yourself with people who take and never give, you're going to end up exhausted and miserable. You must remind yourself how much you matter and why you deserve to be treated every bit as well as you treat other people. Don't forget it!

THOUGHTS BECOME THINGS

It's estimated that we have over six thousand thoughts a day, and plenty of these are good thoughts, so choose to dwell on them. If you find yourself going down negative rabbit holes, it can be helpful to have reliable devices in your mental health locker to pull you back out again.

Finding what works for you is a gamechanger. If you haven't yet figured out what helps your mental health when you have a wobble, the next few pages will give you a few simple techniques to try.

These techniques might not help everyone and there is no shame in speaking to a mental health specialist if you want to get a bit more clarity or advice. We're all here to help each other out, right?

REPLACE NEGATIVE THOUGHTS
WITH POSITIVE ONES

This method of self-care sounds ridiculously simple, but it works! If you start to think you're never going to get your work done on time, flip that belief and replace it with something like, 'If I plan my time well and stay chill, I'll get it done no problem.' Bizarrely, you can literally change your mind using your thoughts. It's called neuroplasticity – the way in which our brain can rewire itself.

One of the best techniques, when you feel negative thoughts creeping in, is to imagine what you'd say to a friend who was thinking the same thing. You would want to comfort them and make them feel as good as possible, right? So do the same to yourself.

If you master your negative thoughts, you can become the calmest, happiest version of yourself. This version of you will radiate MCE because you'll be able to focus on putting yourself first.

MEDITATION

It has been proven that regular meditation decreases anxiety and fatigue, and also has the added benefit of improving attention and memory. Meditation may feel like it takes a while to master, but any meditation you do will be helpful, whether you have tons of thoughts flooding into your head or you're easily able to master moments of silent clarity. There is no right or wrong way to meditate. Trying it is the most important thing. Even if it's just two minutes here and ten minutes there, it all helps. And you can do it as many times a day as you like, whether you're stressed or just fancy feeling a bit more zenned out.

Follow the simple tips on the next page to get started:

Grab a chair to sit on, or a cushion or pillow if you'd rather be on the floor.

Close your eyes to help your mind stay focused and start by taking some long, deep breaths.

Count to five seconds as you breathe in, hold for five seconds and then exhale for five seconds. Imagine breathing in positivity as you inhale and fill your stomach with your breath. Release any negative thoughts as you exhale and let your shoulders drop.

Notice what thoughts come in. It's common to have more thoughts racing around your head than ever when you first begin to meditate, but that doesn't mean you're doing it wrong.

If you find you have the same thoughts coming in over and over again, imagine those thoughts floating up to the sky and being swept away by the breeze.

If your wandering mind starts driving you a bit crazy, just keep coming back to your breath and concentrate on how it feels to breathe in and out.

Now focus on your body. Scan your body slowly. Can you feel anything in the tips of your toes? Work your way up your feet and legs, noting how they feel. Keep going until you get all the way to your head. How does your body feel in this moment?

When you feel ready, slowly open your eyes and give yourself a few minutes to acclimatise. There's no rush to get up – wait until the time feels right.

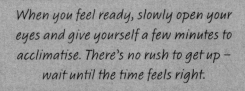

BREATHE

Breathing techniques can calm stress and panic by putting your body into a state of relaxation. Breath is an incredibly powerful natural healer, and it doesn't cost a penny. Did you know that the average person breathes in and out over twenty-three thousand times a day? So you've already got this skill down.

There are loads of different breathing practices to try, but why not start with a few simple techniques to get you started. Unlike meditation, you do these breathing techniques with your eyes open, so you can do them anywhere, anytime, and no one needs to know.

As with meditation, there is no right or wrong here. Try the practice that resonates with you and which you feel the most benefit from. Any kind of healing needs to align with you so listen to your instincts.

HOW TO ... BREATHE WITH PURPOSE

Breathing with purpose is about slowing down your mind so that you can re-energise yourself or completely relax. It's often described as 'active meditation' and is said to help us disconnect from our minds and allow ourselves to be guided by our hearts and souls, so it's great if your head is foggy or you're finding it difficult to decide about something.

Stressed? Try the 5 breaths technique

Humans usually breathe at a rate of around 12 to 20 breaths per minute. The 5 breaths technique, also known as 'coherent breathing', aims to slow that rate down so you can achieve a complete sense of calm.

It's very simple to do. Simply take a deep, slow breath for 10 seconds, then release for two seconds. Repeat this four more times so that you're taking 5 long breaths within a minute. Try it for a minute to start with and then add on a minute each day.

Trying to relax? Try the 4-7-8 method

The 4-7-8 method is great if you're feeling angry, anxious or triggered, and it can also be used at night if you're having problems nodding off to sleep. It releases excess energy from the body as well as negative thoughts, so it's spot on if your body is feeling wired too.

Breathe in through your nose for four seconds then hold your breath for seven seconds. Finally, exhale for eight seconds in one really long relaxing breath. Repeat at least four times but carry on for as long as you want too.

Need an energy burst? Box breathe your way to a boost

If you've got work or studying to do and you just can't find any energy, try box breathing. Kick off the process by breathing out and releasing all the air from your lungs. Then breathe in for four seconds, hold for four, breathe out for four and hold for four again. To really feel the effects, continue for a minimum of five minutes. This is also called the 4-4-4-4 technique – now you know why.

YOU DO NOT HAVE TO GO FULL YOGI TO RELAX

Meditation and breathwork are excellent ways to relax but they are not the *only* ways to relieve stress. We don't have to go all *Eat, Pray, Love* when it comes to finding our best selves. Sometimes we just need to find new ways to let all our emotions out.

Walk, run, cycle, drive or take whatever mode of transport you'd like to the top of a hill and SCREAM. Tell the world why you're angry and let it all out. This is also great fun to do with a friend and directly into the wind. Just don't do it anywhere near other people; they deserve their peace too.

They're cliché for a reason, but bubble baths are the perfect place to chill out. Throw in some bath salts and a colourful bath bomb and soak until you're wrinkly (or the water's cold). Shower steamers are a great alternative if you don't have a bath or hate the idea of one.

In true MCE style, go and stand outside in a downpour and let the rain wash over you. We don't usually like getting caught in a shower but when you're feeling stressed or emotional, there is something healing about standing in the rain and letting it all out. It really will wash your worries away.

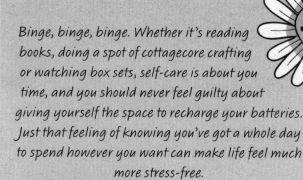

Binge, binge, binge. Whether it's reading books, doing a spot of cottagecore crafting or watching box sets, self-care is about you time, and you should never feel guilty about giving yourself the space to recharge your batteries. Just that feeling of knowing you've got a whole day to spend however you want can make life feel much more stress-free.

MOVE YOUR BODY

We're not all natural athletes and that's fine, but even light exercise like yoga, Pilates or walking can improve mental health by increasing the production of endorphins – your brain's feel-good neurotransmitters. Exercise is good for reducing depression, anxiety and negative mood. It also improves self-esteem and cognitive function and can help with symptoms of social withdrawal.

HOW TO . . . WORK OUT WHAT KIND OF EXERCISE YOU LOVE

There are two kinds of people in this world: those who would rather go for a run than binge-watch their favourite show with a pizza, and those who wouldn't. It may not be quite as cut-and-dry as that, but quite often you either love hitting the gym or you don't. Not all of us are a budding Lara Croft, but there are ways we can get moving.

Hot girl walk – The hot girl walk is the exercise trend of the moment. Yes, it involves walking, but it's also about exercising your mind, because the best self-improvement works from the inside out. The basic rules are that you walk several miles a day focusing on positive thoughts, thinking about the things you want to achieve and are grateful for and how great you feel in your own skin. It's not about losing weight; it's about toning up your mind with good beliefs and getting over any fear of being alone with your thoughts. It helps build confidence and get that all-important vitamin D (if the weather's on your side!).

Get jumping! – Skipping only costs the price of a rope and it's a lot of fun. Although this is a high intensity exercise, it's easy to get absorbed and you'll soon be trying to remaster the playground tricks you used to know.

Get stepping – all our nineties heroines were stepping into shape with their leg warmers and headbands. Why not grab your own sweat-band and get stepping to the beat!

Start small – Try to fit in just three twenty-minute exercise sessions a week. That's all it takes to have a good routine. You don't have to be doing the same exercises. Mix it up. Try as many new things as possible until you find something that makes you go, 'You know what? I'm not hating this.'

Find a fitness buddy – They don't have to be *Baywatch* Pamela Anderson, just find a friend who is also looking to up their fitness game. Having someone you're accountable to can make all the difference. Meet in the park in the morning and go for a walk whilst having a chat. You'll be surprised how quickly the time goes by when you've got someone by your side.

Blast the tunes – Make a playlist of all your favourite upbeat songs, turn your speakers on, crank the volume up and dance! You can literally dance your troubles away.

MINDFULNESS

Mindfulness has been doing the rounds for years now for a very good reason: it works. It may sound a bit worthy, but honestly, it's worth the hype. All you're doing is stopping for a few minutes a day and doing nothing. Could it be any easier?

HOW TO . . . PRACTISE MINDFULNESS

Mindfulness works by drowning out the noise of the world and letting you concentrate on what's really going on inside. It's crucial to take a step back and appreciate just how wonderful the world is. Essentially, it's about pulling our energy back and getting ourselves into a better place.

It may sound a lot like meditation, but there is one big difference. Mindfulness is the awareness of 'things', while the goal of meditation is not to be aware of anything. Mindfulness = focused mind, meditation = clear mind.

Mindfulness is all about the moment. The one that is happening right NOW. Notice how your book or phone feels in your hands. What can you hear around you? Birds singing? Someone shouting in the street? What can you smell? Is someone cooking? Is it your perfume or cologne? Take a deep breath and absorb it all. Have you noticed that you feel a bit calmer already?

You can do this practice anytime, anywhere. Trust your feelings and let your mind wonder with your five senses. Some emotions may pop up that you're not expecting, but that doesn't mean they're not OK. When you finish the practice, take a moment to refamiliarise yourself with the space you're in. Smile. Research has found that even faking a smile can lift your mood. So there is some truth in 'fake it until you make it'.

CHAPTER 6

THE ME I
WANT TO BE

YOUR MCE TOOLKIT – JOURNALING

As you come to the end of your main character journey, there is one more thing you need to master before you release all that protagonist energy into that world, and that is journaling.

Much like mindfulness, journaling keeps you in the moment and allows you some all-important time to yourself to dig into how you're feeling. Once you find your inner voice, reaching your goals is going to be a breeze, and that's why keeping a journal is such an essential part of this journey. You don't have to write all your secrets like Bridget Jones, but journaling will help you to reflect on your growth and take control of your own narrative.

It's common for us to have to put on different faces to the outside world. Even if we're crying inside, we feel we have to smile to the rest of the world. It may be that the only time you can feel like your authentic self is when you're with your

family, your closest friends, your partner or the person who knows you better than anyone else ever possibly could – you. Even then, it can be hard to work out our own thoughts when we have so many of them and life is a constant barrage of information. At times, we're almost told how to think.

That's why journaling is like a best friend that doesn't judge or talk back. It helps us work through the noise in our heads and find the comfort and peace we need from our thoughts.

Your journal is your sanctuary

As you go on this journey of self-discovery, it's helpful to keep note of your progress and any reflections you make. This book has asked you to question a lot about yourself and your intentions, and writing down the answers to all of these questions in a journal helps you encapsulate the journey you've been on and give you one place to look back on it. Putting yourself first does not happen overnight and you may forget some stages along the way. Use a journal as a chronicle of this journey and a reminder of how far you've come.

Journaling is a powerful tool in changing your mindset. Taking the time to write down and work through your feelings can actually lower your blood pressure, which helps strengthen your immune system. It can also help you to regulate your emotions and process difficult moments more easily. In summary, journaling is an incredibly positive experience and it even increases our memory capacity so we can't forget how to put ourselves first in a hurry.

Your journal, your way

There are no rules when it comes to journaling. If you haven't ever written a journal before, the most important thing you can do is get started. Even if you only write one line to begin with, that's OK. Remember, no one is going to see it apart from you, so no one is going to judge. And you must, must, must not judge yourself (one of the main rules of self-care).

Who cares if your writing is a bit scrawly because you're writing so fast you just want to get it out? It's for your eyes and your eyes only, so forget about censoring it or using your best handwriting. The more you share, the better you'll feel, so let it all spill out on to the page.

Journaling doesn't just have to be a rundown of what you've done that day, either. There are so many possibilities. Here are some questions you could ask yourself to kick off your journal. It's time to get deep and discover more about yourself.

What are my short- and long-term goals?

What matters most to me in life?

Who are my safe space people?

What habits would I like to challenge or change?

What are my biggest strengths?

What makes me feel stressed or worried?

What makes me laugh?

What would I like to learn more about?

What comforts me?

What makes me cry?

What is my biggest wish?

What are my values and the things I believe in and am passionate about?

How can I appreciate myself more?

What do I care too much about?

What are my favourite and least favourite parts of my day?

What are my inner critic's most annoying sayings?

How do I show myself compassion?

BULLET JOURNALING FOR ANXIOUS MINDS

Bullet journaling is a technique you can use to keep track of your life. It's best to use a proper diary for this because it can serve as a good reminder of what you did and when. It helps you track habits and goals without you having to write down a lot and it's a great technique for quickly clearing an anxious mind.

Try to answer these questions below as quickly as you can.

 Bedtime routines – What time did you go to bed and what time did you get up? How many hours' sleep have you had? How did that make you feel?

 Social life – Where did you go today? With whom? What did you do? Did you enjoy it? Would you go again?

Screen time – Did you spend time on your phone today? What did you do?

 Health – How are you feeling today? Have you felt the same way throughout the day? What would make you feel better?

 Mood – What emotions did you feel today? What caused those emotions?

 Goals – What are your goals for the rest of the day? What are your goals for tomorrow? How can you achieve them?

HOW DO YOU FEEL?
BY BULLET JOURNALING, YOU CAN
QUICKLY SEE HOW DIFFERENT THINGS
THROUGHOUT YOUR DAY CAN ALTER AND
AFFECT YOUR OVERALL MOOD AND
ACTIONS. IT'S A GOOD WAY TO
ROUND OFF THE DAY OR, IF YOU'RE FEELING
ANXIOUS, HELP YOU WORK THROUGH
THE CAUSE OF THIS WORRY
AND DISPEL IT.

DEAR FUTURE ME

Another important tool in your self-reflection toolkit is imagining what your future romanticised life looks like. You've probably heard of people writing emails to themselves that they'll receive in five, ten or fifteen years. We're going to do something similar here. Instead of focusing on where you're going to live, what job you might have and whether you've found the perfect partner, this letter needs to be full of goals that celebrate the little moments in life.

Consider what brings you joy in everyday life as you start to write. How would you like to feel about yourself? What are the highlights of your day? What do you value most in your life? What do you hope the next few years will teach you?

Take time to truly consider how you want your future self to be living, thinking and feeling, not what material objects or societal expectations they've achieved.

Now, read it back twice and really take in what you've said. That's the love and understanding you deserve. Keep it somewhere safe so that you can reread it whenever you need encouragement.

GET GRATEFUL

Putting yourself first also means reflecting on the journey you've taken and being thankful for the lessons you've learnt along the way. A great way to do this is by practising gratitude.

People who practise gratitude daily are said to be happier, more compassionate, kinder and healthier. In the most simplistic terms, gratitude works by shifting your thinking from the things that have gone wrong during your day to the things that have gone right.

It's super easy to practise gratitude. You can either write down or say out loud the things you're grateful for, whether it's a small moment like having a good hair day or a big moment like landing a new job or getting a great grade for a paper. Even if you just write one or two things you're grateful for each day, it can turn your day around by making you focus on the achievements rather than the failures.

GRATITUDE LETTER

Another surefire way to lift your spirits is to be grateful to someone else. Sometimes a random stranger can make our day by saying something sweet, or you may be lucky enough to be on the receiving end of an anonymous random act of kindness.

Or maybe a friend or family member has gone out of their way for you but you feel too embarrassed to thank them. A great way to show your gratitude is by writing them a letter.

The idea is that you write a letter telling them how much you appreciate what they did and how it made you feel. It's a nice way of realising just how thankful and lucky you are that people do nice things for you. It will also make you feel good because a) you've bothered to write the letter and b) it shows how worthy you are of people treating you well.

Take time to thank those people in your life who actively put you first. There's a lot to learn from them.

you make me feel...

WHY COMPARISON SUCKS (AND HOW TO STOP DOING IT)

If there's one thing guaranteed to make you miserable, it's the horror of comparison. Nothing good can ever come from comparing yourself to someone else, because no one is completely perfect no matter what other people may say.

Never assume someone is happier than you just because they have a certain quality you crave. We've all experienced the feeling of wanting something someone else has and it can quickly become an obsession. You need to remember that something you may disregard or even hate about yourself is a source of great jealousy for someone else. Appreciate yourself, because someone else wishes they were just like you.

It is OK to feel jealous. Envy is a very normal human feeling and everyone feels it from time to time. Just don't let it take over your life. Unless you stop comparing yourself to your peers, you will never truly feel happy with yourself. If you know you're good enough without designer clothes or the latest iPhone, the envy you feel will be no more than a fleeting moment rather than something that spins around your head all day telling you you're not good enough.

Someone who looks like they've got it all may have a rubbish home life and could have spent years learning how to put on an 'everything is great' act. Unless you've got X-ray vision and can see how they really feel, you will have no idea.

We only ever see people's highlight reels, not the stuff that goes on when no one else is around. Everyone has something to deal with.

Have you ever noticed how we all have a very bad habit of comparing up instead of down, too? If you've ever come second in a competition, you've probably asked yourself why you didn't come first, and those irritating 'it's because you're a loser' whispers start echoing in your ears. But did you ever look at the person who came third – or the people who didn't come anywhere – and think, 'OK, I did pretty well actually'?

By comparing yourself to others you're definitely not putting yourself first – instead, you're allowing yourself to take a backseat and play the supporting character, which you most certainly are not. Comparing up or down will do you no favours, so ditch the lot.

A good way of dealing with any kind of envy or comparison is to write it down and then rip the piece of paper into tiny pieces and throw them away. This will help you let go of these feelings, never to plague you again.

Once you free yourself from comparison, you free yourself up to be even more of your brilliant authentic self who doesn't feel the need to be like anyone else. If anything, people will want to be like you!

DROP THE JUDGEMENT

Stop judging others and you will stop judging yourself.

People who are truly at peace with themselves don't put others down to make themselves feel better. If you're happy with who you are, why would you even need to put other people down?

Instead of making you feel better because you can see someone else's imperfections, when you judge someone or criticise them it bounces back on you and makes you feel rubbish, so the only person you're truly hurting is yourself.

This isn't a blame game and if you are in the habit of pulling other people apart, it's a learned behaviour that you can work on – and it's so worth doing that work.

The chances are, if you're being judgemental of other people, it's an old, ingrained habit and you're probably doing the same to yourself without even realising it.

Next time you find yourself criticising someone, stop and ask yourself why. Not in a 'well, it's because they're wearing awful shoes' way, but question why you felt the need to dig them out in that way. Are you feeling a bit rubbish about yourself? Do you feel jealous of them in some way? Once you can get to the bottom of the reason you're doing it, you can start to break the pattern and stop it.

Awareness is key, otherwise you could find yourself still doing it well into old age, and what a waste of time would that be. By being kinder to others you will be kinder to yourself, guaranteed. A critical mind doesn't just look outwards, it looks inwards, and that's feeding your inner critic.

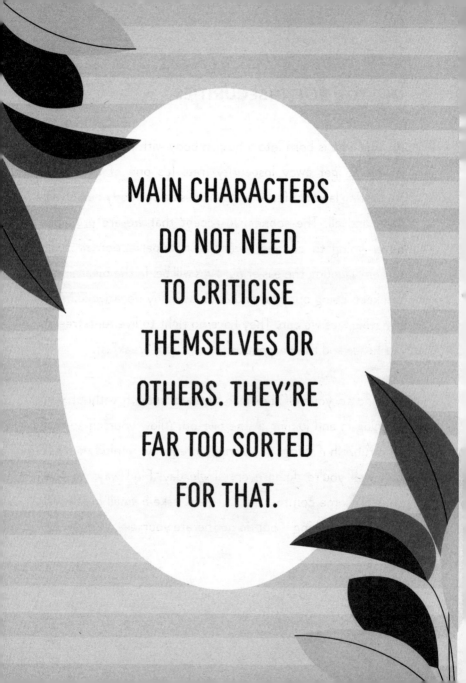

MAIN CHARACTERS
DO NOT NEED
TO CRITICISE
THEMSELVES OR
OTHERS. THEY'RE
FAR TOO SORTED
FOR THAT.

OFF YOU POP, INSECURITIES

No one who is born into a human body with human feelings is able to get away insecurity-free. It's one of the more frustrating laws of life. All we can do is be perfectly ourselves, flaws and all. The sooner we accept that we are probably never going to conquer every fear, imperfection or self-esteem vacuum, the easier our lives will be. In the meantime? We keep doing our best and ditch as many negative learned behaviours as we can. They have no right to live rent-free in our heads and then expect us to buy them breakfast.

Be kind to yourself. Life can be hard enough without you jumping in and joining in the pile-on. Allow yourself to feel a bit rubbish if things go wrong, but equally, remind yourself how well you're doing every single day. Find ways to give yourself some comfort, ask for help, take a small break and do some breathing – but do not berate yourself.

Insecurities are pointless. Harsh, but true.

They don't keep you safe, they keep you small.

They are messages you've picked up during your lifetime and 99.9% of them have no basis. Being aware of them is the first hurdle and it may be painful to become conscious of how many negative thoughts you're letting rule your life. They've likely become so second nature that you don't even realise you're thinking them.

YOU NEED TO BECOME THE CEO OF YOUR MIND AND KEEP THE INSECURITIES AT BAY.

FLIP YOUR FLAWS

There is no such thing as a 'right' way when it comes to how you look, only what society tells us. Flaws are always in fashion and scars are beautiful and tell the story of your life.

Can you spot the really obvious word in imperfections?

(Major clue: It's perfect.) Yep, imperfections are perfect too.

What do you see when you look in the mirror? That spot that appeared overnight completely uninvited? Move your gaze away and focus on the things that are beautiful about you: your uniquely coloured eyes, your gorgeous natural lip colour, your freckles that have come out to say hello now it's sunny (do you know how many people wish they had freckles?), your hair that drives you mad but others would kill for, the crows' feet you have from smiling so much.

ections

Make your fabulousness your focal point and stop looking at the things you wish you could change. There is no need. I bet someone somewhere wishes they looked just like you or envies the way your skin glows without the need for even a slick of foundation. You have qualities people strive for and you didn't even have to do anything to get them.

When you stop and think about it, isn't it ludicrous that there is such a thing as 'trends' when it comes to beauty and body shapes? We're born the way we are and we can't all fit into the latest 'perfect' body. If you follow the crowd and do what everyone else is doing, how are you ever going to stand out as a true individual?

Who you are and how well you treat people will always be on-trend. No matter what is going on externally, from your clothes to your hair to your body, your kindness, compassion and inner strength will always shine through.

In the same way that there is no such thing as perfect, there is also no such thing as normal. Normal is just so . . . normal! The things that make you stand out stop you from being boring. Life, looks and experiences can be messy, but if we approach them with love and self-acceptance, everything changes. That's when you start being your true main character self.

YOU ARE ENOUGH!

You've come a long way on this journey of self-discovery and you've taken more than a couple of steps to harness your MCE. You're already the author of your story and now you're armed with a whole book full of useful tools to help remind you how brilliant you are every day.

It's time to truly commit to loving yourself. To paraphrase RuPaul: how can you expect anyone to love you if you don't love yourself?

Hopefully the journey to self-love has already begun for you and you're getting to grips with just how important a person you are.

It might take time, but if in doubt, just remember:

Be kinder to yourself

Don't judge yourself

Rely on yourself one hundred per cent

Stop comparing
yourself to others

Put yourself first

Believe in yourself

Don't allow others
to treat you badly

Kick self-doubt's ass

Respect yourself

Keep working on yourself and it will all come. And
most importantly, don't give up! This is a marathon, not a
sprint, and your journey to self-acceptance won't happen
overnight. Just remember that you are complete and
can be happy just as you are.

NOW GET OUT THERE AND START **ROMANTICISING YOUR LIFE,** BECAUSE THIS IS THE YEAR THAT **YOU PUT YOURSELF FIRST** AND START ACTING LIKE THE **MAIN CHARACTER** YOU WERE ALWAYS MEANT TO BE!

Your dreams are within reach – master the magic of manifesting and bring them to life.

This book is a beginner's guide, perfect for anyone curious about the philosophy and practice of manifesting but unsure where to start. In just 10 easy steps, you'll create a manifestation plan to shape your future.

The world is discovering the power of manifesting techniques. With this beautiful, practical guide in hand, now you'll be able to achieve your goals, realise your potential and live the life of your dreams.